HOW TO LEARN PYTHON IN 100 MINUTES

Practical Guide for Only Beginners

Rohit Shinde

Seattle Digital Publications

INTRODUCTION

Hello guys the intention behind creating this book is when I was learning C language as my first programming language. The experience was so scary and demotivating. I think Many of you also experienced the same, later on I realized that learning very old programming language like C doesn't make any sense.

Therefore, I decided to skip C language and was searching for something which is easy and has real life use which will help my career as well as love for programming. After researching finally, I found Python. after reading and practicing some stuff of python, I understood that this is the thing which I was desperately searching for, it took me around 6 months to understand and master most of the things in python. Also, my confidence level was very much increased. Its Complete lie that our teachers and seniors tell that you must choose your 1st programming language as C or C++, its basic and all that!!!!

I don't believe in that! Python is very much modern and is very High in demand. Anyone who don't have much computer background can easily learn python in no time. For everyone wish to learn programming my advice is forgot everything and just Learn Python. This book is created only for those who wish to learn programming but don't know where to start?. I tried my best to make this book simple and less theoretical. Specifically, in programming I believe that only practice will make you best programmer not lots of theory and concepts.

Please do me favor if you liked this book Please don't forgot to review and give 5-star rating to this book on amazon. It helps to become Bestseller on Amazon.

"All the best for your Python Journey."

HOW TO USE THIS BOOK

"Repetition is key to Success"

This book is intended to learn faster python programming. In this book I have given sample code for every chapter. Just practice it in your Python Editor to get most out of it. write and modify every code at least 10 times and see the results, observe every line, What errors you face? Try to rectify it by own.

In programming Problem solving attitude is very important. Make minor changes & see the difference.

1,2,3,4 these are just a line numbers Please don't write it in python editor. Whenever you see symbol (#) and some sentences those are called comments in python. It's like description that what specific line does.

Remember Every programming language can be only learned by

practicing and understanding that what went right? and what went wrong? never afraid to make mistakes. every one does the mistakes. Don't procrastinate, block your time for only learning python. At the end of the book, I have given a link to download a file of all programs used in this book.

ABOUT AUTHOR

Rohit Shinde is the Bestselling author of the book 'How to Conquer the Brain'. This book Climbed to the number #6 spot on the 'Amazon Best Seller list'. He is also the Founder of 'Seattle Digital Publications' and has published over 20 best-selling books of different Authors till date. He is an investor and trading consultant for Top 50 Cryptocurrency. He is a

Python programmer by passion. Also, earnest researcher in the field of Artificial Intelligence, Rohit is the kind of person who has multiple skill-sets and strongly believes on continuous learning. he truly enjoys his work and that sincerity is then reflected, in every work area.

ABOUT CO–AUTHOR

Prof. Ashish P. Ramdasi was born in Osmanabad, Maharashtra, India in 1986.He received the B.E. degree in Computer Science and Engineering from B.A.M.U. university Aurangabad, India and M.Tech from J.N.T.U. Hyderabad ,India. He is research Scholar at H.I.T.S. Chennai, India. His current research interest includes Data Mining, Text Mining, Information

Retrieval, Machine Learning. He has been with the department of Computer Engineering, Sinhgad Academy of Engineering, Pune, where he is working as an Assistant Professor. He has 8 years of experience in teaching. He has published more than 20 papers in National/International journals and has participated in conferences to enhance the knowledge of a specific domain. He was coordinator of more than 10 workshops of different domains. Being a coordinator of IIT Bombay

Spoken Tutorial, He has got the opportunity to enhance the knowledge of students through arranging different language courses. He has teaching expertise in Data Structure, Digital Electronics, Object Oriented Programming, Computer Security and Data Mining.

CONTENTS

WHY PYTHON?

There are many programming languages in the market and in this Book, I'm going to tell you why Python is the best among all of them and why you should actually go for it. so, get ready to fall in love with Python! let us start, Python which is extremely simple and easy to learn, since it closely similar to English language. it is a very powerful language and it takes absolutely no skills to learn Python. Python is free and open source. it is a high-level language where, one does not need to bother about low-level you can simply write your code in English and Python will convert it into lower-level. also, python is an interpreted language where machine reads and interprets the code wearing all the arrows are checked during the runtime. python has a very large community so if you have any doubt at any technical issue you can see helps and thousands of Python community members on forums Twitter, Facebook, Q&A sites pretty much everywhere now. if you compare Python with any other programming language such as C, C++, Java, PHP or anything python has outshine among all its peers.

In Python you don't have to deal with complex syntax for example if you want to print simple hello

world program in java you have to write these five lines.

CODE:

```
1.  public classHelloWorld{
2.  public static void main(String[] args){
3.  System.out.println("Hello World");
4.  }
5.  }
```

Whereas in Python just one line is sufficient to print hello world

CODE:

```
1.  print("Hello World")
```

that's yet. it's that simple.

Let's know one by one some of the coolest features and applications of python in tech industry

1)Simple Clean and Easy to Learn:

Simplicity of the code which makes the best suit for beginners, Python is for everyone no matter you are 8-year child or 50-year adult, you can learn python in no time. No prerequisites are required!

2)Portable and Extensible:

Portability of Python I mean python is supported by the most platforms present in industry today. It could be a Windows platform, it could be Macintosh or Linux everybody loves python.

In Python you can completely integrate your Java as well as .net components and even if you wish you can also invoke C and C++ libraries as well therefore you can perform cross language operations with Python. With this Python is extremely extensible with most of the programming languages.

3)Web Development:

Python has range of frameworks for developing website. Now the most popular frameworks available in Python are **Django**, **flask**, **pylons** and **web2py**. In fact, all frameworks are written in Python and as the core reason which makes the code a lot faster and stable. Once you start using these frameworks you will never look back to PHP or any other web development programming language. Now with Python you can also do Scraping which is nothing but fetching details from any other website and storing it in your local system. you will also be impressed as many websites such as Google, Instagram were built on these frameworks only therefore, Python is majorly used in the web development.

4)Artificial intelligence & Machine Learning:

So artificial intelligence is the next big development in the tech world. Now when it is combined with libraries such as "scikit-learn", Python has the ability to do complex calculations with just a single statement. More libraries such as "Karas" and Google's "Tensorflow". Artificial intelligence you can actually make a machine mimic the human brain which has the power to think analyze and make decisions on it. Also we have libraries such as OpenCV that helps in image recognition such as computer vision. You can detect a face or a color and apart from image recognition. You can also detect a character or a handwriting everything is available in Python. So, all this is a part of AI and machine learning so artificial intelligence is the broader concept of machines being able to carry out tasks in a way that we consider smart and hence you can also boost up the overall productivity of the company by saving their time and money and all this can be achieved using Python.

5)Computer Graphics:

Python is largely used in small large online or offline projects. It is used to build GUI which stands for Graphical User Interface I call it NEXT--NEXT--FINISH Applications that we use in windows machines. We use python in game development so "tkinter" is the standard GUI library for Python. Python when combined with tkinter it provides a fast and easy way to create GUI application.

6)Data Science:

So python is the leading language for many data scientists. Now for years Academy scholars and researchers were using the very famous MATLAB language for scientific research. now that all started to change with the release of the numerical engines such as "numpy" and "pandas" python also deals with the tabular matrix as well as statistical data and it also visualizes it with popular libraries, such as "matplotlib" and "Seabourn". so, imagine it guys you have large amount of data let's say terabytes or petabytes of data and using Python you can easily gain insights out of it. so, this is how Python is majorly use in the data science domain.

7)Pythons popularity and High Salary:

It's all well and all the features look pretty interesting but what about the pay?, so Python engineers have highest salary in the industry. So the average Python developer salary in the United States is approximately $103,492 per year and if you see the trend Python is still there and has a strong spike in popularity over the last one year.

There are many big players in the industry who have been using Python from quite a long time now here is Google who is actually using Python for web searches. Then we have YouTube which is largely written in Python. and many other companies such as Instagram, NASA, Dropbox, Facebook, Tesla and many more, so I have just listed a few companies but a lot of companies uses Python. Python is ideal and it is completely capable of doing the job.

INSTALLATION OF PYTHON

To play with python first you need python software and packages to get install on your computer. like any other software installation, python's installation is damn easy.

Visit https://www.python.org/downloads/

Just download latest version of python from above official website according to your operating system, if you are using linux based system then you don't need to install python, most linux based distributions comes python preinstalled.

Once you downloaded python just double click it, as most of the users are considered as windows users, I will guide you how to install python on windows based operating systems.

Click on Next and Select Add python.exe to path>>Entire feature will be install on local hard drive.

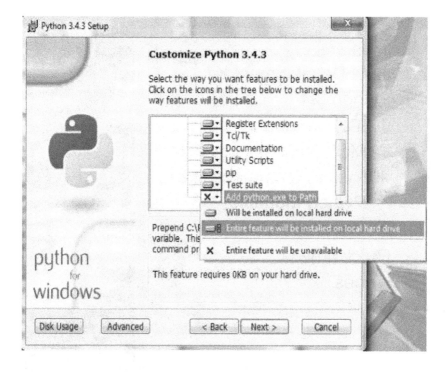

Now just follow Next it will smoothly take you to end of the installation. Now python should be ready and running for you.

Once you see python installed in your start menu, you will see two options IDLE & Python (Command Line). the difference between both are IDLE has graphical user interface. Which is best for beginners. Command line option is for Expert users.

FIRST BABY STEP INTO PYTHON PROGRAMMING

Now in this step we are completely ready to explore whole new world of Unlimited possibilities. Simple Practice that will kick start on how to write program in python. To do that Just Open Python IDLE from start menu, our Goal is to print "Hello World!" text on the screen.

1. **All you need to write a single line of code that is**
```
print("Hello World!")
```

Now Once You Write above code hit Enter, you shall see output below the code.

You Successfully Wrote Your First Python program. Now Let's Rapidly Get started,

I observed that lots of programming books, are filled with only theory and less practical stuff, my approach behind this book is to give you most of the stuff practical and very less theory. I agree that Theory is important to understand but my motive is to Get things done as much as possible in less time.

Sometimes limited information is good, at end of the day only practise will help you to grow and move forward rather than having only information.

WORKING WITH ADVANCE PYTHON FEATURES

As we seen in previous chapter we wrote a simple hello world program in IDLE platform or we can call it as python shell. Writing code in shell is great way to learn python. You just need to press ENTER in order to execute one line of code. But what about when we write more

than one line of code? In this scenario we need notepad like editor to perform this job. This allow you as a programmer to flawlessly write many lines of code blocks and run entire block of code once.

Python provides built-in editor, you just need to open python IDLE CLICK on File>>New File, this will create a python file remember that every file created in python is under **.py** file extension. Once you Create a file you are ready to write as much code you want. To get output of code you must save the file in your local hard drive. After saving the file just click on run module or press **F5** button. Once you do that your code will be run and you will see window popping up showing your Output of code. There are many editors available on Web some of them are Notepad++, **Pycharm**(recommended), sublime text editor and many more.

VARIABLES

"You Can Store Anything Using Variables"

This is the thing which you will use most of the times in programming, Variables are used to allocate and store information in computer memory.

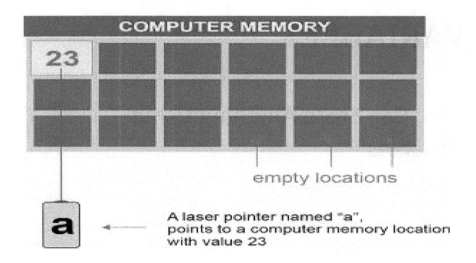

Here are 3 things we are going to use when declaring variables:

1) Identifier

2)Assignment Operator

3)Value

identifier ⟶ **a = 23** ⟵ value

↑

Assignment operator

In Python IDLE
Code:

```
1. a=23
```

Press Enter, In Memory "a" identifier assigned value "23"

Now type "a" and Press Enter. You Will see the output as "23". In This Way We declare Variable in Python

Code:

```
1. name = "python"
2. print(name)
```

BASIC MATH

In python there are bunch of arithmetic operator used for calculation of numbers.

Symbol	Name	Example	Output
+	Addition	5+2	7
–	Subtraction	5-2	3
*	Multiplication	5*2	10
/	Division	5/2	2.5
%	Modulus	5%2	1
**	Exponent	5**2	25
//	Floor division	5//2	2

You can Practice above operators using variables

Code :

```
1.a=20
2.b=10
3.a+b
4.a-b
5.a*b
```

PLAYING WITH STRINGS

In English language there many words and sentences, and its nothing but collection of characters and in python which we call as string. String is always covered with " or '(double or single quotation mark). You can manipulate or play with any character. Using its index values. Remember Every index counts from 0.

```
name = "My Name is Mike"
```

INDEXING

0	1	2	3	4	5	6	7	8	9	10	11	12	13	14
-15	-14	-13	-12	-11	-10	-9	-8	-7	-6	-5	-4	-3	-2	-1

Code:

```
1. string= "My Name is Mike"
2.  string[0]
```

o/p: 'M'

Now Just replace 0 with any other number and see the difference.

Program for Combining two strings:

Code:

```
1. string1="python is very "
2. string2="easy"
3. print(string1+string2)
```

Program to Embed a String in Output:

Code:

```
1. char1 = "Always Remember,"
2. char2= "You have Infinite Power"
3. print("%s %s %s" % ('I like the qu
   ote', char1, char2))
```

Program to Get Rid of Newlines:

```
1. print("I don't like ",end="")
2. print("newlines")
```

Program To print a string multiple time:

```
1. print('\n'"Newlines" * 5)
```

LIST

List is one of the most used and very flexible datatype used in python. It is simple collection of values, separated by comma and embedded within square brackets. List allows you to create a list of values and manipulate them.

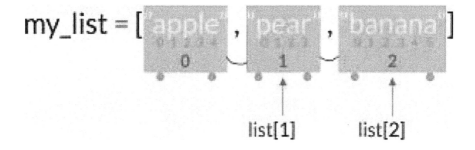

Let's make Simple Grocery list:

Code:

```
1. grocery_list = ['Juice', 'Tea', 'R
   ice', 'Sugar']
2. print('The first item is', grocery
   _list[1])
```

o/p: **The first item is Tea**

Tip: Index always starts form Zero not One

```
1. # empty list
2. my_list = []
3.
4. # list of integers
5. my_list = [1, 2, 3]
6.
7. # list with mixed datatypes
8. my_list = [1, "Hello", 3.4]
```

Program to change values of List:

```
1. grocery_list[0] = "Noodles"
2. print(grocery_list)
```

Program to slice the list:

```
1. grocery_list = ['Juice', 'Tea', 'R
   ice', 'Sugar']
2. print(grocery_list[1:3])
```

Tip: [1:3] Means it will print only 1st to 2nd index values, it will not print 3rd Index.

Program to create List of Lists:

```
1. grocery_list = ['Juice', 'Tea', 'R
   ice', 'Sugar']
2. other_events = ['Meetings', 'Excer
   cise', 'Bank']
3. to_do_list = [other_events, grocer
   y_list]
4. print(to_do_list)
```

Program to Get the first item in the first list:

```
1. grocery_list = ['Juice', 'Tea', 'R
   ice', 'Sugar']
2. other_events = ['Meetings', 'Excer
   cise', 'Bank']
3. to_do_list = [other_events, grocer
   y_list]
4. print(to_do_list[1][1])
```

Tip: As We Know Index Starts from Zero, grocery list **will be 1st List and** other events **will be zero. In 4th line of code, 1st bracket [1] Indicates** grocery list
And 2nd bracket [1] indicates 'Tea'

Program to Add Values to list using append:

```
1. grocery_list.append('onions')
2. print(grocery_list)
```

Program to Remove Values from list using remove:

```
1. grocery_list.remove('onions')
2. print(grocery_list)
```

DICTIONARIES:

A dictionary is a collection of KEYS and VALUES, which works same like List. In List we have seen that there is only number as Index to indicate string characters, but in dictionary values can be indicated by any type of number or character. In dictionary values are indicated by Unique Key.

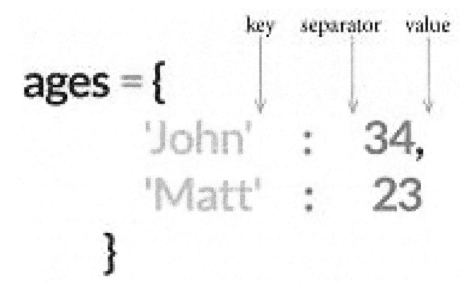

Code:

```
1. best_criket_players = {'India' : '
   Sachin Tendulkar',
2. 'Srilanka' : 'K.Sangakkara',
3. 'Australia' : 'Adam Gilchrist',
4. 'South Africa' : 'Jacques Kallis'}

5. print(best_criket_players['India']
   )
```

Program to Delete an entry:

```
1. best_criket_players = {'India' : '
   Sachin Tendulkar',
2. 'Srilanka' : 'K.Sangakkara',
3. 'Australia' : 'Adam Gilchrist',
4. 'South Africa' : 'Jacques Kallis'}

5. del best_criket_players['Srilanka'
   ]
6. print(best_criket_players)
```

Program to Replace a value:

```
1.best_criket_players = {'India' : '
  Sachin Tendulkar',
2.'Srilanka' : 'K.Sangakkara',
3.'Australia' : 'Adam Gilchrist',
4.'South Africa' : 'Jacques Kallis'}

5.best_criket_players['India'] ='MS
  Dhoni'
6.print(best_criket_players)
```

Program to print number of items in the dictionary:

```
1.best_criket_players = {'India' : '
  Sachin Tendulkar',
2.'Srilanka' : 'K.Sangakkara',
3.'Australia' : 'Adam Gilchrist',
4.'South Africa' : 'Jacques Kallis'}

5.print(len(best_criket_players))
```

Program to print list of dictionary keys and values:

```
1. best_criket_players = {'India' : '
   Sachin Tendulkar',
2. 'Srilanka' : 'K.Sangakkara',
3. 'Australia' : 'Adam Gilchrist',
4. 'South Africa' : 'Jacques Kallis'}

5. print(best_criket_players.keys())

6. print(best_criket_players.values()
   )
```

CONDITIONALS

Till So far, we have learned lots of uses of simple statements and operations, but the main purpose of any programming language is to have some type of logic and decision making.

In Python there are If, Else and Elif statements used to perform different actions based on conditions.

To Validate the Conditions in Python we use **Comparison Operators like: ==, !=, >, <, >=, <=**

Operator	Description
==	Equals Too
!=	Not Equals Too
>	Greater Than
<	Less Than
>=	Greater Than or Equals Too
<=	Less Than or Equals Too

if Statement:

The simple if statement will execute code if a condition is met. While writing the code in Editor you will notice white spaces are created, this is used to group blocks of code in python. If white spaces are not properly maintained you may get unexpected indent error or invalid syntax error while running the code.

Code:

```
1.age = 30
2.if age > 16 :
3.print('You are old enough to drive ')
```

if /else statement:

Use an if/else statement if you want to execute different code regardless of whether the condition is met or not.

Code:

```
1.age = 21
2.if age > 16 :
3.  print('You are old enough to Dri
   ve')
4.else :
5.     print('You are not old enough
   to drive')
```

elif Statement:

If you want to check for multiple conditions use elif, If the first matches it won't check other conditions that follow.

Code:

```
1. age = 15
2. if age >= 21 :
3.  print('You are old enough to driv
    e a Truck')
4. elif age >=16 :
5.  print('You are old enough to driv
    e a Car')
6. else :
7.  print('You are not old enough to
    drive')
```

Conditions with Logical Operators:

Here we are going combine conditions with logical operators to compare two different values.

Logical Operators: **"and"**, **"or"**, **"not"**

Code:

```
1. marks = 87#we define Marks=87
2. if ((marks >= 40) and (marks <= 69
   )): #if marks Greater than 40 and
   less than 69
3.  print("Congratulations You are Pa
   ss")
4. elif (marks == 70) or (marks >= 71
   ): #if marks equals to 70 or great
   er than 71
5.  print("You Achieved Distinction G
   rade")
6. elif not(marks == 39): #if marks e
   quals to 39
7.  print("You are Fail")
```

Tip: Once any condition is met, code will no longer check other conditions.

LOOPING

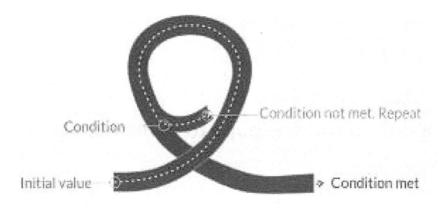

Condition

Condition not met. Repeat

Initial value

Condition met

In python there are two types of loops that you can use regularly

1) For
2) While

1) For:

For loop allows you to perform an action a set number of times. loop must be defined using *"for"* keyword.

Now we will print 10 numbers between 40 to 50 (but not 50)

Code:

```
1. for x in range(40, 50):
2. print(x)
```

Program to use for loops to cycle through a list:

```
1. grocery_list = ['Juice', 'Tomatoes
   ', 'Potatoes', 'Bananas']
2. for y in grocery_list:
3. print(y)
```

Program to sort greater number form list:

```
1. num_list = [1, 2, 5, 6, 7, 8, 9]

2. for number in num_list:
3. print('looking at:'+str(number))

4. if number >6:
5. print ("Too big:" +str(number)+"!
   ")
```

2) While loop

While loops are used when you don't know time how many times you'll have to loop. *"while"* keyword is used to start a loop. In this you will see packages and modules. It's simply a readymade code.

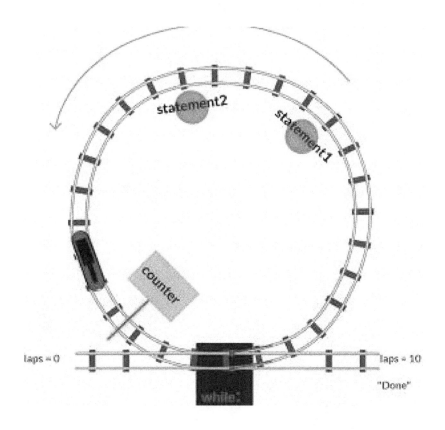

Code:

```
1. import random #random is Python
   Module (see last chapter)
2. random_num = random.randrange(0,10
   0)
3. while (random_num != 15):
4.   print(random_num)
5. random_num = random.randrange(0,10
   0)
```

SIMPLE FUNCTIONS:

In programming to gain more flexibility and greater productivity we use functions to only write once a specific operational code block and use it in many times where ever you want by calling function name.

Function starts form "**def**" keyword called as define, the function name and   parameters

Code:

```
1.def addNumbers(fNum, sNum) :
2.     sumNum = fNum + sNum
3.     return sumNum
4.print(addNumbers(1,4))
```

o/p: 5

USER INPUT

Getting input from, the user is interactive way to communicate with program. It's very easy to take input from user and process the information in python.
Code:

```
1.import sys
2.print('What is your name?')
3.#user types "Rohit"
4.name = sys.stdin.readline()
5.print('Hello', name)
```

FILE I/O

As a computer user we daily encounter with various files like simple text file, music file, video file and lot more. Generally, we use computer programs to open and close the file with few double clicks. We use programs like notepad to open a simple text file. likewise, in python you can also open and do operations on file with little code. there are two modes available in python read and write mode. Now we will do some file operations and see how we can easily manipulate files.

Program to create simple text file:

```
1.file=open("textfile.txt", "wb")
```

Program to display the name of file:

```
1.file=open("textfile.txt", "wb")
2.print(file.name)
```

Program to write some text in file :

```
1.file=open("textfile.txt", "wb")
  #wb is for write mode
2.file.write(bytes("This is Sample T
  ext", 'UTF-8'))
```

Program to close a file:

```
1.file=open("textfile.txt", "wb")
2.file.write(bytes("This is Sample T
  ext", 'UTF-8'))
3.file.close()
```

Program to read information from file:

```
1.apple= open("textfile.txt", "r+")#
  "r+" is for read mode
2.text_in_file = apple.read()#apple
  is just variable name
3. print(text_in_file)
```

CONCATENATION:

Concatenation is used to join two or more strings into one, it's called concatenation. To Join more strings, we use + operator.

cone + cat + ten + ate

Code:

```
1. all_strings= "cone" + "cat" + "ten"
   + "ate"
2. print(all_strings)
```

PACKAGES & MODULES:

Why Python is becoming so popular? One of the reason is its simplicity, but another shining part is its prebuilt modules and packages. A module is simple python file which contains classes, functions & statements.

In short you don't need to write or invent completely new code or function to do specific tasks, this

work is already done by millions of python developers worldwide. Packages are collection of modules used to keep large amount of code well organized Python has very rich library of modules and packages for any programming operations. If in any other programming language there is complex 1000 lines of code written to do specific task, then in python by importing modules in code we can easily eliminate 70-80% of unnecessary code. This ability of python increases productivity of developer and makes python code simple and neat. Now we will use datetime module to do operations with date and time.

To access functionalities of datetime module just write below code at starting of your python file

```
1.import datetime
```

now you can access all module features using dot(.) notation

```
1.import datetime
2.print(datetime.datetime.now())
3. #o/p: 2018-06-21 21:44:19.780163 (it contains in
   series of current year, month, day, hour, minutes,
   seconds, and milliseconds)
```

CONCLUSION AND DOWNLOADS

I Hope You Understood the various elements of Python programming. Every language has some collection of letters after understanding nature of every letter we are able speak & write like that, every chapter is a letter. When you practice well then you can create anything using python. First draft of this Book was around 240 pages. In that draft, I included everything from basic to very much advance. but after that I realised the purpose of book was to learn python in less time, not to make it confusing and hard.

So, I eliminated very important concepts like Object Oriented Programming, Polymorphism, constructors and many more. When you master this book then it's no big deal to learn advance python by your Own.

Here is all programs list which are used in this book. Please Click Below to Download.

Click here to Download All Programs

Thanks a lot for buying this book, I'd love to know how was your learning Journey?

Please do me favor if you liked this book Please don't forgot to review and give 5-star rating to this book on amazon.

Please Click Here to Write a Review....

CREDITS

1. Learn Python Visually

2. Python for Dummies

3. http://python.org

4. http://w3schools.com

Checkout Our Other Books

❖How To Conquer The Brain: Learn How to Take Full Control Over Your Behaviour Patterns, Changing Habits, Neural Pathways

❖Cyber Security HandBook :: Cyber Domain is Unforgiving Be Prepared

❖Cyber Case Studies: Better to Learn from Other's Mistakes, Than to Commit the Same and be Sorry Later

❖DETECTION OF WEB:: Top 20 Cyber Crime Attacks Explained